SIERRA LEONE
LEONE
NARROW GAUGE

Philip Beale and Vic Mitchell

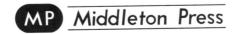

MP Middleton Press

Cover pictures:

Front : Hunslet 2-6-2T no.45 of 1920 shunts at the Government Wharf at Freetown in 1941. One of the fleet of 30 is now to be found in Wales. (Dr. P.Ransome Wallis)

Back: Garratts were used exclusively on the 3ft 6ins mineral main line until the advent of diesels in 1955. Two of the four were photographed soon afterwards, near Marampa. No. 5 is nearest; the other has lost its leading tank. (Prof. H.P.White)

About the authors

Philip Beale is a Cambridge history graduate who spent part of his career in West Africa. As a result of his interest in postal history, he has written extensively on the subject, notably **The Postal Service of Sierra Leone**.

Vic Mitchell is co-author and publisher of most of the railway albums shown on the last page of this volume. He has had a life-long interest in narrow gauge lines and was one of the founders of the scheme to revive the Festiniog Railway.

The two writers had a long acquaintance through Methodism, but it was to be many years before they learnt of their special interests. Aptly, this was during a chance meeting on a train journey to their local station at Haslemere.

Philip has drawn upon his collection and those of other members of the British West Africa Study Circle, while Vic has sourced more recent material through his associates in the narrow gauge world. They hope that the result will bring pleasure to those who missed the opportunity to visit the unique lines described herein.

Those wishing to know more about the West Africa Study Circle are invited to write to the membership secretary, Peter Duggan, 75 Alexandra Road, Reading, RG1 5PS.

Published April 2004

ISBN 1 904474 28 4

© Middleton Press, 2004

Design   David Pede
Typesetting   Barbara Mitchell

Published by
          Middleton Press
          Easebourne Lane
          Midhurst, West Sussex
          GU29 9AZ
Tel: 01730 813169
Fax: 01730 812601
Email: info@middletonpress.co.uk
www.middletonpress.co.uk

Printed & bound by MPG Books Ltd, Bodmin, Cornwall

CONTENTS

I. Map of the railways in the 1950s. The word "Government" has been inserted in the title of the main railway throughout this book, to distinguish it from Mineral Railway. The Mountain Railway is shown on Map X in section 2. (Railway Magazine)

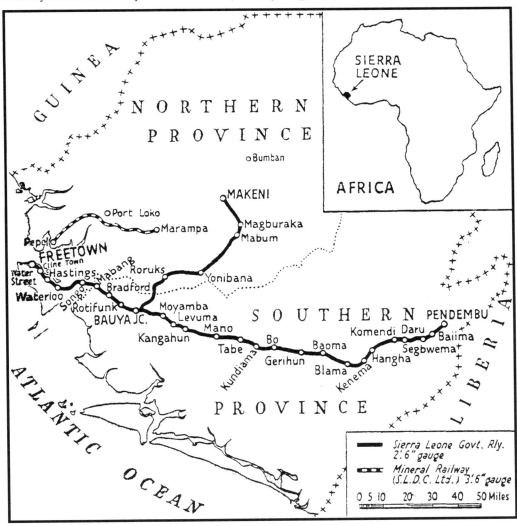

INDEX TO SLGR STATIONS

ACKNOWLEDGEMENTS

We are grateful to many of those mentioned in the credits for their assistance and also to G.Croughton, P.Mosse, J.Powell, Dr. J.Rainbow and Mr D. & Dr. S.Salter.

Our wives have been most supportive in this project. Both are Barbara - God bless them.

We also pay tribute to those service personnel who took the photographs dated 1941-43. Not only did they often breach the restrictions on photography, but they sometimes used their gas mask bags to carry their cameras instead of respirators, thus risking their lives for our ultimate benefit.

Introduction
HISTORICAL SETTING

The country of Sierra Leone, or Lion Mountains, was named by the first Portuguese explorers who saw the land from the sea. They were looking for a route to India and for the source of the gold that came across the Sahara Desert. Soon trade started in ivory, slaves, camwood and beeswax using manufactured goods for exchange and then iron bars as currency. English Trading Companies became active but no settlements were made until 1787 when 411 mainly black people sailed from Plymouth. They were settled on land purchased from local chiefs. A Sierra Leone Company, founded by Granville Sharp, William Wilberforce and others to promote trade and oppose slavery, was established by Act of Parliament in 1791. Former slaves were brought from Nova Scotia and others, the Maroons, came from Jamaica. In 1807, an Act was passed forbidding the slave trade and in the next year Sierra Leone became a British Crown Colony, a place to which captured slave ships could be taken and former slaves set free in Freetown.

The Colony was on the peninsula and behind it lay a far larger area later called the Protectorate whose boundaries were finally agreed with France and Liberia at the end of the nineteenth century. The railway was planned to open the Protectorate to trade and to bring together the different peoples who lived there. It led to the construction of telegraph lines and Post Offices with roads leading to the railway stations.

During both world wars the fine harbour of Freetown was much used for transporting troops and, in the second war particularly, as an anti-submarine base. Sierra Leone provided troops for campaigns in East Africa and the Far East. By stages the country developed its own government and on 27th April 1961 it became an independent state.

GEOGRAPHICAL SETTING

Sierra Leone Government Railway

The 227½ mile-long main line ran roughly east-west across the middle of the Southern Province of the country, with a 104 mile-long branch running north into the Northern Province at Kamabai.

The capital, Freetown, is situated on the northern flank of the Colony area peaks which rise to well over 2000ft. The route runs to the north of these mountains for 20 miles. However most of the main line was at under 250ft above sea level for its first 135 miles, as was the branch. The eastern section was at under 500ft, except for the final 50 miles.

Numerous deeply incised river valleys are crossed, notably the Jong, the Sewa and the Moa. The underlying geology of the western section was mostly Laterite (a soft Sandstone-like mineral), while the eastern part was predominantly on Granite. This included areas containing Chromite ore.

The lines were built mostly through closed forest, although agricultural land increased in time. The rainfall was in the range of 100 to 125ins per annum, although higher near the coast. The population density per square mile was 75 to 100 in most areas served by the main line, but less on the branch.

Mountain Railway

This climbed steeply from the port of Freetown to an altitude of 820ft in 5½ miles. Hill Station is a residential area with a more agreeable climate than that on the coast and with a lower insect population. The community is located at the northern end of a rocky outcrop, which measures about 20 by 5 miles and peaks at 2912 ft at Picket Hill. The area provided many recreational pleasures and good quality housing.

Sierra Leone Development Company

Its line was built to convey ironstone from extensive quarries at Marampa on a 52½ mile long journey to the port of Pepel, which is 15 miles across the Sierra Leone River estuary from Freetown. Those gradients against the load were limited to 1 in 125.

One major river is crossed (Port Loko Creek) near the middle of the route, but a small water course at its western end resulted in the harbour being built on an island. This half of the route was laid largely on swamp.

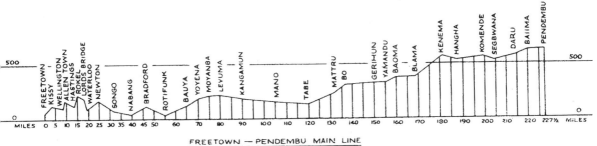

FREETOWN — PENDEMBU MAIN LINE

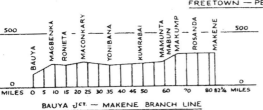

BAUYA JCT. — MAKENE BRANCH LINE

II. Simplified gradient profiles, with the 500ft altitude indicated. The diagram is after 1930, but includes some earlier spellings.

HISTORICAL BACKGROUND

Sierra Leone Government Railway

Surveying started in 1893, but it was not until 25th May 1896 that the first engine was steamed on the construction work, which began at Cline Town. The gauge of 2ft 6ins was chosen and trains were running to Wellington by March 1897. A trial trip to Waterloo was made on 1st April 1898, but civil unrest further inland brought construction work to a halt and the railway was used for troop movements to prevent an invasion of the Colony. By August, it was possible to run excursions from Freetown to Waterloo and a regular Saturdays-only service began in October 1898.

The first passenger train to Songo was on 18th March 1899, but the official opening was on May 1st. The last of the security forces had returned in February. However, a further uprising delayed work in 1900 and the route to Moyamba did not open until 1st October 1901. The line to Bo (136 miles) officially came into use on 17th January 1903, after the tribal chiefs had been placated and shown the benefits that the railway could bring.

Baiima (220 miles) was reached on 22nd August 1905. The year 1907 brought the commencement of a system of tramways in or beside the new roads in the rural areas. The first was from Baiima to Pendembu, but this was soon converted to a railway and trains reached the eastern terminus, Pendembu (227 miles), on 29th June 1908.

Various branch tramways were laid, notably one from Bauya (64 miles) north to Roruks, a distance of 16 miles. These were a great success and they were termed railways from 1911. They totalled 212 miles by 1912.

The route from Bauya was extended by 16 miles to Yonibana on 1st October 1912. It was further lengthened to Magburaka on 10th February 1913, making the branch 66 miles long. It reached 83 miles when it was opened to Makeni on 12th January 1915. The extension to Kamabai on 12th February 1916 made the branch total 103½ miles, but this section was short lived and closed on 3rd July 1930, the work on a further extension to Baga having been abandoned. These sections were largely converted to roads.

The wartime years of 1939 to 1945 had seen a revival, but also a deterioration in the railway stock and track. In only four years since 1927 had the railway made a profit. The Hangha chromite mine developed before the war of 1939 was closed in 1963 which was a further blow and the Government faced the question of whether to continue with subsidies. The internal air service was a new competitor. Road transport proved to be quicker and cheaper.

Reduction in mileage began in 1968 with the closure of the Makeni Branch. Pendembu to Kenema followed in 1971, Kenema to Bo in 1973 and the final train ran in November 1974. Most of the track was lifted in 1975.

Passengers used almost exclusively the first half of the line from the coast. Reluctantly the decision was taken to phase out the railway. It had served the country well and a modern map shows how it had determined the construction of towns and trade. All the provincial capitals were on the railway line. It has had a permanent effect on the development of the modern country of Sierra Leone.

The principal freight commodities are given opposite for sample years.

	1927	1938	1949
	tons	tons	tons
Local traffic			
Native Rice	6206	5351	5401
Native Timber	330	670	3673
Fire Wood	1275	159	-
Dried Fish	-	678	549
Imports			
Native Foodstuffs	2512	3230	7240
Building Materials	333	750	2093
Cotton Goods	692	549	298
Hardware	366	1204	788
Kerosene	656	660	1326
Motor Spirit	204	471	1622
Provisions	1095	899	536
Salt	3608	2566	3323
Cement	314	1272	5336
Other Merchandise	3533	2624	2042
Exports			
Palm Kernels	39,537	33,986	40,924
Kola Nuts	2463	1382	622
Ginger	1375	2952	1077
Palm Oil	2503	1663	2438

Most of the palm kernels were exported as a source of compounds for the production of glycerine, margarine, soap and lubricants.

1.   Temporary bridges were constructed from local wood in order to speed tracklaying and major civil engineering works. This example is "up country" in 1903 and carries one of the first batch of Hunslet 0-6-0Ts. (P.Konec coll.)

2.   An early postcard by Lisk-Carew recorded the basic goods handling procedures and the nature of those involved. At first there was much local hostility to the railway within the Protectorate. (F.Walton coll.)

Mountain Railway

Although part of the SLGR, this suburban railway is usually considered separately, both historically and operationally. It was built mainly for the carriage of European residents and opened for an excursion on Easter Monday, 4th April 1904. Some military barracks were built near the line, these adding to its meagre revenue.

The passengers were among the first to have motor cars and consequently the line had an early demise, closing completely on 28th February 1929.

Sierra Leone Development Company

The company was formed on 20th September 1930 and the railway was completed in February 1933, along with a deep channel and harbour.

The wider gauge of 3ft 6ins was chosen for the heavy traffic planned, this gauge being in extensive use for main lines in Southern Africa. An axle load of 13 tons was adopted to enable each wagon to carry 30 tons. Three passing loops were laid, these providing five sections of roughly equal length.

The business was very successful and updating in the mid-1950s brought dieselisation and an increased axle limit of 16 tons to allow 50 tons in each wagon. (The limit on the SLGR was only 5 tons).

Closure seems to have been in about 1976, but some travel permits were issued in January 1985. Since military rule was enforced, it has been impossible to obtain precise records.

SLGR PASSENGER SERVICES

Excursions were run from Freetown to Waterloo on 8th and 11th April 1898 and a regular service began on Saturdays from October of that year.

The Rotifunk - Moyamba section opened with one train per day, excepting Sundays, but a local service was maintained at the west end of the route.

Upon opening to Bo, one train was provided each weekday, but, within eight weeks, two of these trips each week ended at Moyamba.

A weekday service was introduced over the entire system in 1914, when all main line trains terminated at Bo. Through passengers had to stay overnight there. Trains were never operated on Sundays.

As an economy measure in 1917, the branch and the line east of Bo had only three trains per week. A drop in local traffic resulted in the SLGR starting a bus service between Freetown and Wellington on 28th April 1930. A network of bus routes followed.

There were even greater reductions in World War II, with the line west of Bo having only three trains per week; to the east, and on the branch, there were only two. The figures were six and three from May 1944.

Pendembu received six trains from June 1947 and in 1950 a thrice-weekly express completed the journey from Freetown in a single day. This was in addition to the stopping trains each side of Bo. There was also a commuter train from Waterloo and one from Songo, the latter starting at 3.5am and completing the 32 miles to Freetown at 7.15. Night running of goods trains began in 1950 and passenger coaches were included in them between Freetown and Bo.

By 1955, the SLGR was conveying annually 1.35m passengers at a maximum speed of 20mph and an average of 13, using a fleet of 103 coaches. These had vacuum brakes from 1916; prior to which, three boys applied them manually on each train.

There was a service of one train per day between Freetown and Waterloo still running in April 1974.

SLGR TRAVELLING POST OFFICE

One of the main uses of the railway was to carry the mail. An order was placed in 1906 for datestamps to use in postmarking ordinary mail and oval datestamps for registered letters. They included the words SIERRA LEONE GOVT RAILWAY. The first recorded postmarked envelope is dated September 1907. On 17th October 1912 the official newspaper, *The Gazette*, announced that postage stamps and envelopes would be sold by the postman on the trains between Freetown and Bo at all places where there was no Post Office. By then the Post Office was paying an annual subsidy of £850 to the Railway. There were eight vans under the charge of postmen, each having a compartment for carrying mail bags which were delivered and received at places where there were Post Offices. Mail could be handed to the postman at the other stations and halts.

The SLGR had eight dedicated postal vehicles and received a substantial annual subsidy for their operation. This snap was published in 1962 and shows EIIR by the letter box. (Philatelic Magazine)

In 1914 a large postmark was introduced reading TRAVELLING POST OFFICE FREETOWN - B.O. The maker evidently did not understand that there was a place called BO and must have presumed it meant Branch Office or Box Office, hence the fullstops. Letter boxes had been introduced before 1919 for posting letters on the trains. Mail was also carried by the Mountain Railway to and from Hill Station.

By 1925 there were Post Offices or Postal Agents at most of the stations along the line to Pendembu and on the branch line to Makeni. They could issue Postal Orders and so provided a simple banking system for small traders. Where there was no Post Office or Agent the postman on the train could sell stamps and deal with Postal Orders. A parcel service also operated. Rectangular adhesive labels were brought in for registered mail. The postal service continued throughout both of the world wars, despite many supply difficulties. It served the country well until the closure of the rail system.

A detailed study of the postmarks is included in Frank Walton's *The Postmarks of Sierra Leone,* published by The West Africa Study Circle, and Philip Beale's *The Postal Service of Sierra Leone to 1961,* published by The Royal Philatelic Society.

Postmarked 21st December 1917, this letter carries the faulty TPO postmark of B.O. instead of BO. It had been inspected by the military censor, for security reasons, during World War I. (P.O.Beale coll.)

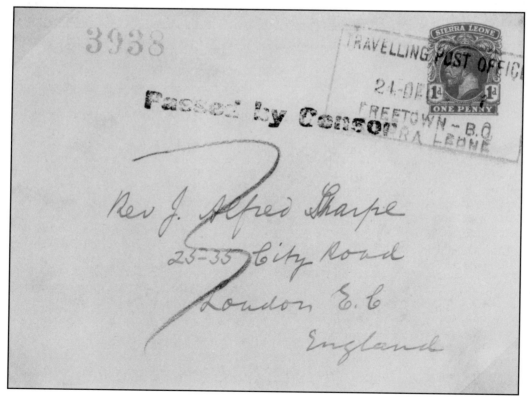

A datestamp from 24th September 1953 includes "TPO". (J.Hossack coll.)

SLGR - OTHER COMMUNICATIONS

A telegraph system was completed between Freetown and Waterloo in November 1898 and was soon made available for public use. It was extended as the railway routes grew.

Telephones were soon also using the wires and these were extended to government offices and official residences. A new exchange was provided in 1915 and the service was made available to the public in 1916, when 13 subscribers were enrolled and the wires extended to Hill Station. There were soon over 1000 miles of wire serving many towns.

Following the closure of the Makeni branch, the telegraph and electric train staff wires were all used for telephone services. As late as 1950, the trunk exchanges were staffed in business hours only and closed for two hours for lunch. Connections to other countries were only made for one hour each day at that time.

The first radio service in West Africa was operated by the SLGR, starting on 7th May 1934. Although having no trains to run, the Railway Department did not close until 30th June 1977 as it performed many other functions, including providing some water supplies.

SLGR - MAKENI BRANCH

III.   This 1925 map shows the tribal boundaries, together with the branch at its optimum when its terminus was at Kamabai (top right). It was cut back in 1930 to Makeni. This place and the junction are spelt with the early version; there were often several alternatives, but we use the final form in each case in this volume.

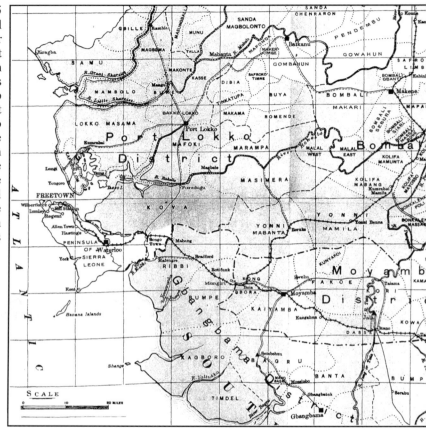

3.   This is the only branch photo that we can locate, but it was simply annotated "Roadside Halt" and so the photographer may not have known his precise position. The locomotive is 4-8-0 no. 181, an Andrew Barclay product of 1944. (Prof. H.P.White)

SLGR LOCOMOTIVES

4.　　No. 1 was one of two 0-6-0Ts built in 1896 by the Hunslet Engine Company for the line. Five more followed in 1902-11 and were numbered 4 and 11-14. The longest serving was no. 14 which survived until 1938. (D.Joy coll.)

5.　　No. 10 was built by Manning Wardle in 1915 for use on the Fourah Bay Harbour construction, but this was abandoned and the engine became the Freetown shunter, known as *Nellie*. Its axle loading was eight tons, three tons more than was allowed on the bridges. It still exists: see picture 4.5. There was one other 0-4-0, this being a saddle tank, which was supplied to the SLGR by Bagnall in 1896. (D.Trevor Rowe)

6.　　　No. 85 was photographed in 1975, prior to preservation in Wales. Similar 2-6-2Ts were supplied by Hunslet in 1898-1920 and numbered 21 to 47. Nos 81-83 followed in 1947 and 84-85 arrived in 1954. They were used mostly in the Freetown area. A batch of six 2-8-0 tender locomotives came from the South Indian Railway during World War II. They were numbered 111 to 116 and had been built by the Swiss SLM in two batches, in 1913 and 1920. They did not last beyond 1947. (R.T.Russell)

7.　　　The fleet of 37 4-8-0s came from different British builders and were of the same basic design. Nos 151 - 156 were from Nasmyth Wilson in 1910-13, nos 157-162 were from Hawthorn Leslie in 1914-15, nos 163-167 were built by North British Locomotive in 1921 and finally there came nos 168-187, which were a mixture of Andrew Barclay and Bagnall products in 1944. (Dr. P.Ransome-Wallis)

8.   The Beyer-Garratt fleet began with nos 50-52, which were constructed by Beyer, Peacock & Co. Ltd in 1926. The 2-6-2 + 2-6-2 arrangement was continued with nos 53-56 in 1928-29 and nos 57-62 in 1942-43. Eight were rebuilt to 2-8-0 + 0-8-2 by the SLGR. No. 62 was photographed in 1943. (F.Birden)

9.   The fleet was enlarged further in 1955-56 when nos 63-76 came into service. They were from the same builder, but were 4-8-2 + 2-8-4. They were an immense success and proved to have the ideal specification for the difficult route. No. 67 was photographed in 1971. Conversion to oil firing began in 1959. (D.Trevor Rowe)

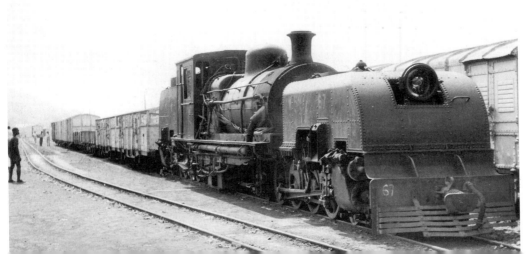

10.   Dieselisation started in 1954 with the delivery of nos 101-103, which were diesel mechanical 0-8-0s of 145hp. Nos 104-108 were similar and followed in 1959-60. All SLGR diesels were from Hudswell Clarke. No. 107 was photographed in 1974; it survives, along with no. 105. It appears to have five axles, but the leading one is a layshaft. (R.T.Russell)

11.   Nos 120-143 were 2-8-2s and arrived between 1958 and 1961. Nos 123 and 133 avoided the scrapman; the latter was photographed in 1977. The diesels were reported to have low reliability initially. This batch had Paxman 225hp engines, with dual Fluidrive transmission. (P.Rowe)

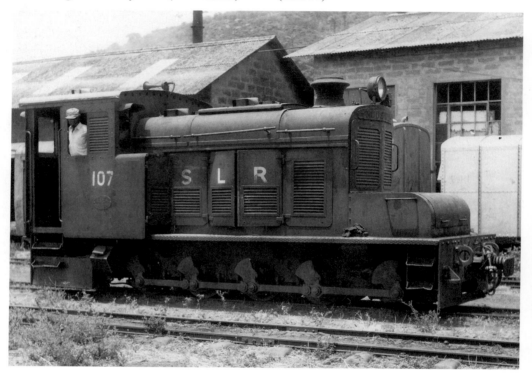

12.   Eight Wickham railcars were supplied from 1949 onwards, but the records of the earlier ones are not available. The first was delivered in 1912. This example is on standard gauge track at the works at Ware in Hertfordshire. (R.R.Darsley coll.)

1. Sierra Leone Government Railway
FREETOWN (WATER STREET)

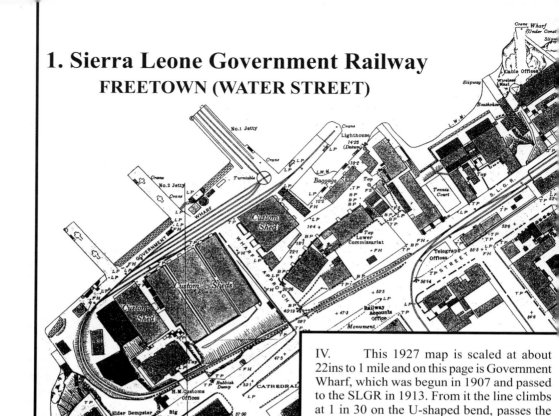

IV.   This 1927 map is scaled at about 22ins to 1 mile and on this page is Government Wharf, which was begun in 1907 and passed to the SLGR in 1913. From it the line climbs at 1 in 30 on the U-shaped bend, passes the cathedral and the 1913 SLGR accounts office,

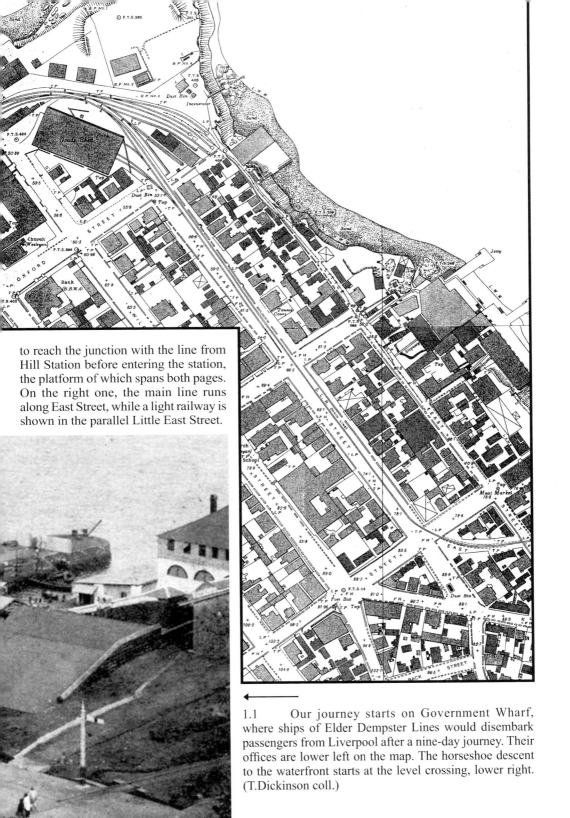

to reach the junction with the line from Hill Station before entering the station, the platform of which spans both pages. On the right one, the main line runs along East Street, while a light railway is shown in the parallel Little East Street.

1.1   Our journey starts on Government Wharf, where ships of Elder Dempster Lines would disembark passengers from Liverpool after a nine-day journey. Their offices are lower left on the map. The horseshoe descent to the waterfront starts at the level crossing, lower right. (T.Dickinson coll.)

1.2   Most trains started from Water Street station until the final years. This postcard view is of the street elevation and in the background is one of the wireless masts marked on the map. (F. Walton coll.)

1.3   Attached to the north elevation was a roof that spanned part of the platform and the adjacent track. Water Street ceased to be an "open" station in 1901 and platform tickets were then issued. No. 171 was an Andrew Barclay 4-8-0 of 1944 and is seen in the late 1950s. A semaphore signal is attached to the stanchion by two bars of steel. It appears to be the only one at this station. (Prof. H.P. White)

1.4   A 1975 record shows iron mesh or sheeting at most windows on the south elevation. Only fragments of the elegant first floor verandah remained. A buffet was opened here in 1945. (R.T. Russell)

1.5　　　The west end is seen in 1975, several years after the two tracks had been lifted from the ground on the left. The station had been closed in about 1969, trains subsequently starting at Cline Town. (R.T.Russell)

→

1.6　　　The building had been restored by 1994 and its Laterite stonework had been painted over. It had become the headquarters for the bus network. (M.Ward/R.R.Darsley coll.)

→

1.7　　　The crowds have moved out of the way of the train as it rounds the curve between the station and East Street, sometime in the late 1960s. It seems that a van has been detached from a train destined for Water Street. (O.Andrew)

EAST OF WATER STREET

←——

1.8 Trains ran in East Street for about ¼ mile. No. 171 is a 1944 Andrew Barclay 4-8-0 and is climbing at 1 in 50 from the terminus. The next view is seconds later. (Prof. H.P.White)

←——

1.9 Assisting at the rear was one of the 2-6-2Ts, used mainly for shunting in the coastal region after the arrival of the Garratts. The two views were taken in the late 1950s. (Prof. H.P.White/ A.C.Mott)

1.10 When this postcard was produced in the early 20th century, there was little road traffic to conflict with the light railway in Little East Street. (F.Walton coll.)

V.   This map overlaps the previous one and includes the goods depot at Susan's Bay. On the right is Nichols Bridge.

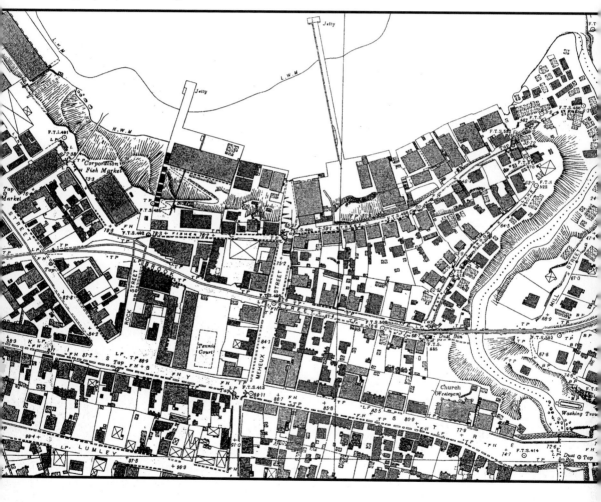

1.11   Susan's Bay was photographed long before the waterfront was developed to the extent shown on the map. The main line is in Brook Street in the right foreground. (T.Dickinson coll.)

1.12   One of the 4-8-0s was recorded on Nichols Bridge, running tender first to Cline Town, where the first turntable was situated. The white panels on the coaches are sun shades. (W.Bickers-Jones coll.)

CLINE TOWN

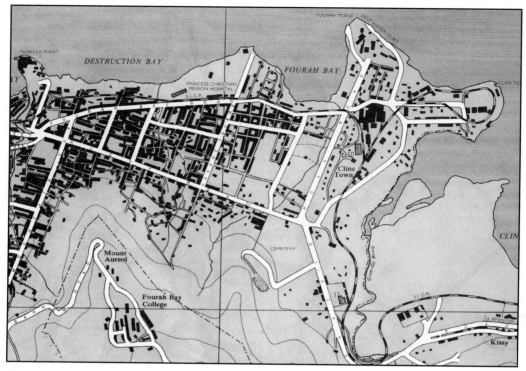

VI.   The map is from around 1950 and is at a scale of about 4ins to 1 mile. Government Wharf is about ½ mile from the left border. On the right are the main wharves that followed the unsuccessful work in Fourah Bay (centre). The railway workshops are in the vee of the tracks; they had been built on part of a racecourse.

1.13   The four-road running shed is right of centre on the next map and this photograph was taken in 1941, as were the next two. The nearest of the 4-8-0s had been built by Hawthorn Leslie in 1915. (Dr. P.Ransome-Wallis)

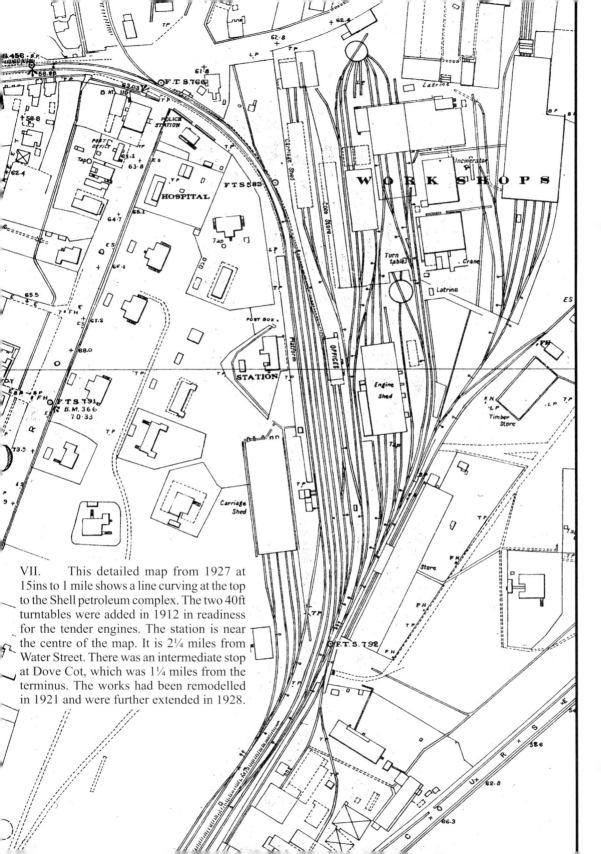

VII.   This detailed map from 1927 at 15ins to 1 mile shows a line curving at the top to the Shell petroleum complex. The two 40ft turntables were added in 1912 in readiness for the tender engines. The station is near the centre of the map. It is 2¼ miles from Water Street. There was an intermediate stop at Dove Cot, which was 1¼ miles from the terminus. The works had been remodelled in 1921 and were further extended in 1928.

1.14   Transport of chromite ore from Hangha began in 1937 with 729 tons, this figure rising to 15,498 tons in 1940. There was great annual fluctuation, a good year being 1946 with 23,404 tons. About 50 such bogie hopper wagons were used for the traffic. (D.J.Mitchell)

1.15   No. 47 was a 2-6-2T from the Hunslet Engine Company in 1920. South Wales coal had been used almost exclusively until World War II, when Nigerian and South African fuel had to be resorted to, with consequent steaming problems. (Dr. P.Ransome-Wallis)

1.16   This is a special train for the RAF, which had established airfields inland at Hastings and Waterloo. The fuselages of some fighter aircraft were conveyed on flat wagons on occasions, with some difficultly. Note the extra cab ventilation.
(Dr. P.Ransome-Wallis)

1.17   Photographed outside the works offices on 14th May 1971 was one of the first Garratts. It was one of the batch to be converted to 2-8-0 + 0-8-2 and unusually carried a nameplate: *Robert Malthus*. He was the chief mechanical engineer who introduced the Garratts. (D.Trevor Rowe)

1.18   Even the 1916 carriage works was well equipped. This is its traverser, which is shown top right on the map. The photograph is from 1974, by which time the premises were in terminal decline. (R.R.Darsley)

1.19   The erecting shop was recorded in 1975 as nature was taking over. A brass foundry was established in 1915 and one for iron and steel followed in 1920. The latter continued to function after the railway closed. (R.T.Russell)

←——————

1.20   A belated attempt to modernise with containers was made in 1968, but such regular traffic ceased soon afterwards, leaving these two examples to be photographed in 1974 on the platform. Freight trains were run "as necessary" in the final years. (R.R.Darsley)

←——————

1.21   We now have five pictures from May 1975, six months after the last special passenger train had run. The remaining serviceable stock stands at the platform alongside the ambulance coach, its white paint peeling and its red cross barely visible. The works office is on the left. (D.J.Mitchell)

1.22   There was much work in progress at the time of closure. The plans to create a National Engineering Centre came to nothing. Diesel no. 134 is on the left and on blocks on the right is 0-4-0 ST no. 10. There was still a works staff of 840 early in 1974, the figure having been over 1000 in steam days. (D.J.Mitchell)

←

1.23   Electric supply is evident; this was completed in 1941. Here we look towards the sea with the platform on the left and one of Shell's tanks in the background. On the right are smaller fuel tanks, together with the wagon frames from which they have been removed. These were used to form the final trains which carried rails lifted from the main line. (D.J.Mitchell)

1.25   We now look inland from beyond the crossover seen in the background of the previous picture. Thus the main line is the centre track. The rearrangement was associated with the construction of a viaduct to ease gradients and curvature. Long trains departing inland were prone to stall on this incline and to have to whistle for assistance from the depot. The smokebox and the wagons were awaiting scrapping. (D.J.Mitchell)

←

1.24   Moving further inland we see one of the few signals on the SLGR. The others were sited on the approach to Water Street and Bo. On the left is the final and lower position of the main line, the earlier line being on the right. (D.J.Mitchell)

1.26   We return for a final look at the coast at Cline Town Docks in April 1974, as rails were approaching the ship, which was loading scrap metal destined for Japan. This deep water harbour came into use in 1951-52. (R.R.Darsley)

VIII.   A later but undated map includes the more direct route south of Cline Town, together with the commercial branches.

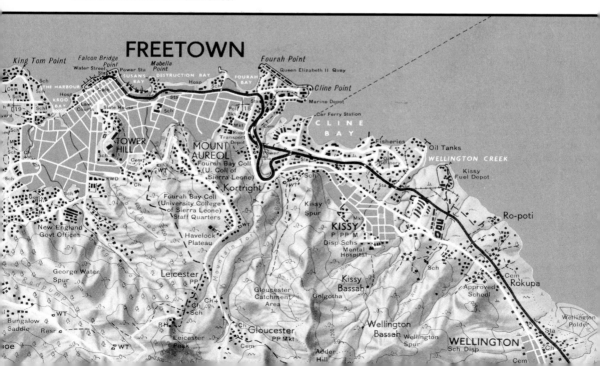

FISHER LANE

1.27   A so-called "Flag station", or request stop, was opened here in 1901, for the benefit of local residents. Owing to the extra demands of World War II, an extensive marshalling yard was laid out in the area. This allowed short freight trains to be worked over the particularly severe gradients on the four miles from Freetown. The large building served as a carriage shed. No. 178 was a Bagnall 4-8-0 of 1948 and is seen on 13th November 1964. (J.Wiseman/R.Dickinson)

1.28   Single line operation was controlled by electrically released tokens, a system employed widely in the UK. The equipment is protected by security mesh at the window and is seen in 1974. (R.R.Darsley)

(left)
1.29   For operational convenience, a running shed was established on the site. Garratt no. 64 was receiving attention on 15th April 1971, although repair work was still undertaken at Cline Town. Alongside is 2-6-2T no 85, which was later to be repatriated. (D.Trevor Rowe)

(lower left)
1.30   The end was nigh when the carriage shed was photographed in May 1974. Restaurant cars had been tried in 1946-48, during which time the total fleet of coaches numbered 84. (R.R.Darsley)

(below)
1.31   This engine shed had been little used in its final years, but on 29th May 1975 there was steam to be seen again as 2-6-2T no. 85 was given a trial run prior to purchase and shipment for use in Wales. (R.T.Russell)

1.32   Kissy station was four miles from Freetown and after leaving it inland-bound trains passed over the six-span Kissy Viaduct. It is seen in 1905. (P.Konec coll.)

WELLINGTON

1.33   Tribal costumes are still commonplace inland. The 2-6-2T is no. 24. The station was seven miles from the terminus and is seen in a postcard view. Nearby market gardens supplied Freetown with vegetables and fruit by rail. (F. Walton coll.)

EAST OF WELLINGTON

1.34   Eleven miles into our journey we cross the slender Orogu Bridge, which was photographed in the 1950s with one of the first batch of Garratts at work. The first crossing of this ravine had been on a six-span structure, 384ft in length. The scenery in this area is spectacular. (R. Wall)

HASTINGS

1.35   Trains travelled 13¼ miles to reach this inland location, the village being ½ mile south of the station. This 1942 photograph was marked "Going-Home-Time for Workmen". They had probably been constructing RAF Hastings. (WLR Archive)

1.36   This photograph is from 1993, by which time most windows had been boarded or blocked up although the building was in residential use. Concrete signs were used widely and were not pilfered, having no secondary use. (M.Ward/R.R.Darsley coll.)

WATERLOO

1.37   Waterloo station was 20 miles from the start of the journey and the local population was 3196 in 1951. A goods train was recorded at an earlier date, along with barrel transport. These were available for hire in 300 and 700 gallon sizes and were used on the roads and narrow tracks in vast quantities. Most were fitted with handles and needed two or four men to move them. (B.McCloy coll.)

> *The train to Bo, he no agree to go,*
> *The train to Bo, he no agree to go,*
> *The engine man dun tire,*
> *The engine no catch fire,*
> *The train to Bo, he no agree to go.*
>
> (one version of a popular local song)

1.38   Two white engineers are sitting in office-style chairs while four black workers are ready to operate the pump trolley. An early surveyor recorded "I travelled by hammock, but my bearers often complained that the ground was very difficult for them".
(B.McCloy coll.)

→

1.39   A 1969 record reveals that little had changed. This view includes the large sliding door that kept secure all parcels in transit. There were market gardens in the area and fresh produce was conveyed to Freetown. The settlement had been founded soon after the famous battle. (O.Andrew)

→

1.40   A 1974 panorama includes the passing loop near the end of which is an open-ended shed. There had earlier been an early morning train from Waterloo for the benefit of those working in Freetown. (R.R.Darsley)

1.41   The last train was operated by Garratt no. 73 and was recorded in sombre circumstances as shadows lengthen. The headboard was produced for the visit of the Queen of Tonga, a few months earlier. Her name was chalked onto the headlamp. The date is 17th November 1974. (WLR Archive)

S. L. R.
Not Transferable
Issued subject to the Conditions and
Regulations in the Railway Tariff
One Bicyclo
Waterloo To
Cline Town
Paid

SONGO

1.42   The arrival of a train always attracted onlookers and traders. No. 123 was recorded with the Pay Train in April 1975. The land from Waterloo via Newton rises all the way to Songo. (R.T.Russell)

1.43   The local permanent way men are ready to set out in May 1975, only months before all traffic ceased. The main line had been relaid with rail at 30lbs/yd in 30ft lengths. We are 32 miles from our starting point. (P.Rowe)

1.44   This is a permanent way hut, Sierra Leone style. Most of the sleepers had been of hardwood imported from the UK, as local timber rotted too quickly. Steel sleepers were used almost universally on the main line from 1935. (P.Rowe)

MABANG

1.45   Local produce stands in the loop of this station, where local enterprise had been at work on the roof to reduce the effect of the sun on the iron sheeting. (W.Bickers-Jones coll.)

BRADFORD

1.46   This station was 48 miles from Freetown and was named after the railway's first resident engineer. This photograph is from 30th April 1975, by which time the only regular train was the weekly Pay Train. This is a special train and at its head is 2-8-2 no. 123. (R.T.Russell)

1.47   A panorama from a departing train shows the casual nature of the level crossings. Note the lack of shadow from the poles due to the sun being directly overhead. (P.Rowe)

ROTIFUNK

1.48   The general ambience of the area is conveyed well in this early postcard view. The location was 55 miles from the terminus and near one of the headwaters of the River Kukuli, which was about 27 miles long. (F.Walton coll.)

1.49   Few early views are dated, but this one was recorded as 1902 and so it may have been the first train to travel this far. (P.Konec coll.)

1.50   This panorama was from the back of one of the last trains to traverse the route. Note that there is a well-worn footpath along it; this was a common sight, despite the trespass regulations. There was dense forest on the next part of the route. (R.T.Russell)

BAUYA JUNCTION

1.51   Sixty four miles from the coast, the station was officially named "Boia Junction" until March 1927, although often spelt "Boya", which reflects its pronunciation. This view shows that a subway was provided under the bay line, although there was only a short walk to the building to avoid using it. (F.Walton coll.)

1.52   A branch train stands in the bay (left), sometime prior to 1924. Also evident is the massive goods shed. A turntable had been added in 1912. A buffet was opened here in 1945. (M.T.Dawe)

→

1.53   This view from the station verandah was dated 30th April 1975 and reveals that three passenger trains could be accommodated simultaneously in the past. The engine shed is in the distance. The train that day was run for the pleasure of a group from Wales purchasing stock and the next two pictures were also from that occasion. (R.T.Russell)

→

1.54   The locomotive being refuelled is no. 123 and in the shed were nos 63, 81 and 133. No. 123 is seen running round its train in the previous picture. In both views it is attached to an engineers coach, which carried a generator to restart the engine, as it had weak batteries. A drop pit had been provided here in 1924. (R.T.Russell)

1.55   One of the vehicles in the train still carried a white notice: LAST TRAIN 17 NOVEMBER 1974, as did those bought for use in Wales. The Pay Train continued as long as there was track to run on. The tank was supplied from a dammed stream using the combination of a waterwheel, an hydraulic ram and a steam engine. (R.T.Russell)

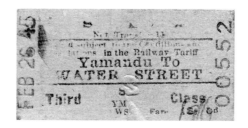

MANO

1.56   This station was on one of the principal roads of the area and was 106 miles from the starting point. It was five stations and more than 40 miles from Bauya Junction. (R.Revell coll.)

1.57   The environs were recorded in April 1974 as the inevitable decline took place. This is an infertile area comprising mainly low shrubs. (R.R.Darsley)

1.58   A number of temporary bridges were built to speed the completion of the railway. This one is listed as "Matuba 1905". Note the office chair on the pump trolley. (P.Konec coll.)

1.59   Bo was the main town on the route, its population being recorded as over 15,000 in 1950. After travelling 136 miles from Freetown, passengers in steam days had to find overnight accommodation here if they wished to proceed further. The postcard was produced in 1904. (P.Konec coll.)

IX.   This map was published in 1953 and shows the relationship of the station to all the necessities of life at that time and also to much undesirable swampland. The scale is 4 ins to 1 mile.

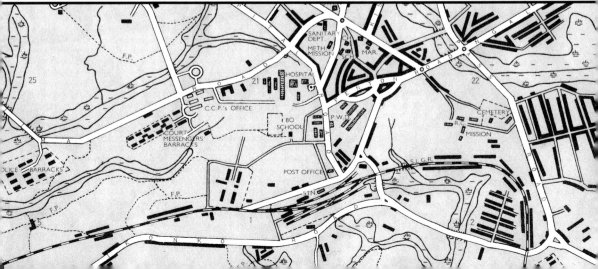

1.60 Bo Rest House was established during World War II to give Army personnel a few days leave. They were conveyed in special trains of the type recorded by Cpl. Hubbard in 1941. It is headed by 4-8-0 no. 156 and is seen during a break on the journey, when locals gathered for handouts. (M.Hubbard coll.)

1.61 An incomplete snap is the first of three pictures from 1968. The shed had been erected in 1911 and its water was supplied by a windpump. (R.Revell)

1.62   Not all the smoke vents on the running shed could be included in this view of the yard from the platform. It seems that car conveyance was not a common practice. The locomotive is one of the 2-6-2Ts and the car is a Skoda Octavia. (R.Revell)

1.63　　　The turntable was provided in 1912 for use by 4-8-0s of the type seen. This example, no. 170, came from Andrew Barclay in 1944; a side view emphasises the large size of the tender. (R.Revell)

EAST OF BO

1.64   The longest bridge in the country was over the River Sewa, 160 miles from Freetown. Overhead conveyors were in use when the construction scene was recorded on 1st April 1904. (P.Konec coll.)

1.65   The test train was photographed later that year, with sacks of local produce at the rear. The six spans totalled 715ft; the river was about 130 miles in length. On the west bank was Baoma station, of which we have no photographs. (P.Konec coll.)

BLAMA

1.66   This rural stop was about nine miles from Sewa Bridge and was the location for an important meeting between Chief Sanosi Jumba and His Excellency General Graves. Blama is in the centre of the palm oil production area. (T.Dickinson coll.)

KENEMA

1.67   The fostering of goodwill with the suspicious and sceptical local residents was a major part of early railway management. This postcard simply states: "Dancing Party at Kennema", using its early spelling. (T.Dickinson coll.)

HANGHA

1.68   Another 1904 panorama and this includes the now familiar propaganda to show the railway as the salvation of the district by conveying its valuable exports. It was also important to show rail-borne inspectors, but mass trespass continued nevertheless. Despatch of chrome ore began from here in October 1937; mining ceased in 1963. (P.Konec coll.)

EAST OF HANGHA

1.69   The bridge over the River Moa was 213 miles from Freetown and the third longest at 632ft. The flags and decorations were out for its crossing by General Graves; he was hauled by 2-6-2T no. 34 of 1903 at 4.0pm on 22nd August 1905. The train was loaded with 50 tons of kernels. (P.O.Beale coll.)

1.70   The Moa Bridge had five long spans, this being an advantage when whole trees were passing under after a deluge of rain. (F.Walton coll.)

SEGBWEMA

1.71   This photograph is from April 1974 and appears to include a locomotive inspection pit and cattle pens. Traffic seems to have ceased in 1971. (R.R.Darsley)

BAIIMA

1.72   We are now 220 miles from the western terminus and seven from the eastern one. The postcard stated: "Baima. Terminus of the Railway Lines". From August 1905 to August 1908, passengers continued their journey by hammock or on foot and goods items were conveyed on the tramway. Trains arrived on alternate days at 4pm, approximately. The final section of the line to be built was mostly about eight miles from the border of Liberia. By 1910 Baiima had a large platform and had attracted many traders. (B.McCloy coll.)

Working Timetables commencing 22nd March 1933. (P.Mosse coll.)

UP **WATER STREET—BO.**

Distance from Water Street.	Distance between Stations.	Stations and Sidings.	1	3		5	7	9	11	13	15	17a	17	19a	21	19	
			Goods.	Goods.	Goods.	Pass.	Pass.	Pass.	Pass.	Goods.	Goods.	Pass.	Pass.	Pass.	Refuse.	Pass.	P
			T. Th. S.	M. W. F.	T. Th. S.		M. W. F.	T. Th. S.		M.W.F.	T. Th. S.	S. O.	S. E.	S. O.		S. E.	
			A.M.	A.M.	A.M.	A.M.	A.M.	A.M.	A.M.	A.M.	A.M.	P.M.	P.M.	P.M.	P.M.	P.M.	P.
M.	M.									...	11.30	12.44	2.10	2.30	...	4.15	5.
		WATER ST. dpt	...	...	...	6.20	7.35	7.35	8.15	...	...	12.47	2.13	2.33	...	4.18	5.
	1¼	Rock Street	...	...	...	6.33	...	...	8.18	...	P	12.49	2.15	2.35	...	4.20	5.
1¼		DOVE COT ... arr	...	...	...	6.35	7.40	7.40	8.20	...	11.35	12.51	2.17	2.37	...	4.22x14	5.
		dpt	...	...	...	6.36	7.46x6	7.46x6	8.21	...	...	12.54	2.20	2.40	...	4:25	5.
	1	Savage Square	...	...	...	6.39	...	...	8.24	...	11.40	12.56	2.22	2.42	...	4.27	5.1
2¼		CLINE TOWN arr	...	...	...	6.41	7.50	7.50	8.26	9.30	11.50	12.57	2.24	2.43x14	3.0	4.32x16 18	
		dpt	4.15	5.30	5.30		7.52	7.52				s	s	s		s	
		Race Course Road										s	s	s		s	
		Kissy Brook								...	...	1.8	2.35	2.54	...	4.43	
	2¼	Fisher Lane	...	...	...	...	8.1	8.1			P.M.						
4¾		KISSY ... arr	P	5.43	5.43	...	8.5	8.5		P	P	1.12	2.39	2.58	P	4.47	
	2¼	dpt	4.28	5.47x2	5.47x2	...	8.7	8.7		9.43	12.3	1.16	2.41x14	3.1	3.27	4.50	
		Rokupa										s	s	s		s	
7		WELLINGTON arr	P	P	5.56	...	8·16	8.16		P	P	1.25	2.50	3.10	3.35	4.58	
		dpt	4.37	5.56	6.5	...	8.18	8.18		9.52	12.12	1.27	2.52	3.11	4.6 x14 16 18	5.0x20	
		Robis										s	s	s		s	
		Upper Allen Town	...	...	...	...	s	s		...	...						
		Lower Allen Town										1.37	3.2	3.21	4.16	5.10	
	6¾	Kossoh Town										s	s	s		5.16	
13¼		HASTINGS ... arr	5.3	6.22	6.31	...	8.40	8.40		...	...	s	s	s	...	5.22	
	6¾	dpt	5.8x2	6.43x6	6.43x6	...	8.43	8.43									
		Rokel	...	...	...	...	s	s		P 10.18x8	P 12.38	1.53	3.18	3.37	...	5.26	
		Devil Hole										1.54x14	3.41 x14 16 18	3.44x16	...	5.28	
20		WATERLOO arr	5.37	P	7.12	...	9.8	9.8		...	...	2.5	3.52	3.55	...	5.39	
		dpt	6.10x6	7.12	7.32	...	9.13x8	9.13		...	...	2.12	3.59	4.2	...	5.46	
		One Mile Village															
	5½	Three Mile Village								10.47	1.7	2.21	4.8	4.11	...	5.55	
25¼		NEWTON ... arr	P	P	7.59	...	9.37	9.37		10.57	1.17x14			4.22	...	5.58x22	
	6½	dpt	6.37	7.39	8.8	...	9.40	9.40						s		s	
														s		s	
32		SONGO arr	7.5	8.7	8.36	...	10.4	10.4		P	P	..	...	4.50	...	6.21	
	8	dpt	7.10	8.13x8	8.46	...	10.9	10.9		11.24	1.44	...	...	4.56	...	6.22	
40		MABANG ... arr	P	P	9.17	...	10.35	10.35		...	...	...	...	s	...	s	
		dpt	7.41	8.44	9.24	...	10.38	10.38		...	...	...	...	s	...	s	
	8	Masanki Siding	...	...	...	...	s	s		11.52	2.12	...	...	5.24x22	...	6.50	
48		BRADFORD arr	8.13	P	9.56	...	11.5	11.5		12.2	2.20x16						
	7¼	dpt	8.20	9.14	10.5	...	11.10	11.10x14		12.33	P						
55¼		ROTIFUNK ... arr	P	9.41	10.32	...	11.35	11.35		12.38x14	2.51						
		dpt	8.49	9.46	10.57x14	...	11.38x14	11.38									
	9									1.10	3.29						
		BAUYA					P.M.			1.15x18	3.41x22						
64¼		JUNCT ... arr	9.25	P	11.33	...	12.8x22	12.8x16		P	4.10						
		dpt	10.0x14	10.21x14	12.20x16	...	12.20x18			1.42x22	4.15						
		Yoyema					s				4.46						
	11½				P.M.												
75¾		MOYAMBA ... arr	10.46	11.7	1.12	...	1.2			2.18							
		dpt	11.13x16	11.15x22	1.21x22	...	1.7			2.25							
		Levuma					s			3.11							
	15½		P.M.	P.M.						3.16							
91¼		KANGAHUN arr	12.14	P	2.35	...	2.2										
	15¼	dpt	12.20x22	12.17	2.54	...	2.5			P							
106½		MANO ... arr	1.29	1.25	4.0	...	3.1	To Makeni		4.17							
	12	dpt	1.40	1.30	4.24	...	3.6										
118¼		TABE ... arr	P	P	5.12	...	3.46			5.24							
	17½	dpt	2.28	2.18	5.27	...	3.50			5.30							
		Mattru					s			P 6.18							
136		**BO** ... arr	3.38	3.28	6.37	...	4.48			7.28							

N.B.—Engine of train 15 will leave Cline Town for Water Street as ordered by Control.
No. 17 crosses No. 14 at Kissy on T.Th. and crosses No. 14 at Hastings on M.W.F.

NOTES.

The following is an index to the abbreviations used in this Working Time-table :—

M. W. F. ... Mondays, Wednesdays and Fridays.

T. Th. S. ... Tuesdays, Thursdays and Saturdays.

S. E. ... ... Saturdays excepted.

S. O. ... ... Saturdays only.

S. ... ... Train stops when required to take up or set down passengers.

P. ... ... Denotes *passing* times where trains are not required to stop for the purpose of dealing with traffic, thus P 10.0.

X. ... ... Trains cross.

MAIN LINE.

UP

BO—PENDEMBU

Distance from Water Street.	Distance between Stations.	Stations and Sidings.		25	27	29	
				Goods.	Pass. T. Th. S.	Goods. M. W. F.	Goods. T. Th. S.
136		**BO**	dpt	A.M. 5.30	A.M. 9.0	A.M. 11.15	NOON 12.0
148½	12½	GERIHUN	arr	6.21	9.43	P.M. 12.6	12.51
			dpt	6.31	9.47	12.11	12.56
155½	7	YAMANDU	arr	6.58	10.10	P	P
			dpt	7.6	10.14	12.38	1.23
159¾	4¼	BAOMA	arr	7.25	10.30	12.57x24	1.42x24
			dpt	7.33	10.35	1.2	1.47
168¾	9	BLAMA	arr	8.9	11.5	1.38x26	2.23
			dpt	8.39	11.10		
181¼	12½	KENEMA	arr	9.30	11.53x24		
			dpt	9.45	11.58		
187½	6¼	HANGHA	arr	10.10x24	12.20		
			dpt	10.30	12.25		
199	11½	KOMENDE	arr	11.16x26	1.3		
			dpt	11.50	1.8		
204½	5½	SEGBWEMA	arr	P.M. 12.12	1.26		
			dpt	12.25	1 31		
	8¾	Moa Siding			S		
213¼		DARU	arr	1.8	2.2		
			dpt	1.18	2.6		
220½	7¼	BAIIMA	arr	1.44	2.28		
			dpt	1.51	2.33		
227½	7	**PENDEMBU**	arr	2.20	3 0		

BRANCH LINE.

BAUYA—MAKENI

Distance From Water Street.	Distance From Bauya.	Distance between Stations	Stations and Sidings.		31	9
					Goods. M.W.F.	Pass. T.TH.S.
			WATER STREET	dpt	A.M. ...	A.M. 7.35
			CLINE TOWN	dpt	...	7.52
			BAUYA JUNCT.	arr		P.M. 12.8
		9¼		dpt	6.10	12.20
73½	9¼		MAGBENKA	arr	6.47	12.51x32
				dpt	7.0	12.54
		11¼	Ronieta			S
84¾	20½		RORUKS	arr	7.56	1.33
				dpt	8.16	1.38
		16¼	Maconkary			S
101	36¾		YONIBANA	arr	9.30x18	2.33
				dpt	9.50	2.38
		12¾	Lever Siding			
113¾	49½		KUMRABAI MAMILA	arr	10.55	3.22
				dpt	11.10	3.25
		12¾	Mamunta	dpt	...	3.58
126½	62¼		MABUM	arr	P.M. 12.16	4.12
				dpt	12.30	4.15
131	66¾	4½	MAGBURAKA	arr	12.47	4.29
				dpt	1.15	4.34
		16	Rosanda			S
147	82¾		**MAKENI**	arr	2.20	5.35

Nos. 31, 30 and 32 must stop for traffic at all intermediate sidings as required.

2. Mountain Railway

X.   This 1925 map includes the entire 5½ mile route from Water Street (right of centre) to Hill Station station. Note the severity of the curves. The stations on the Mountain Railway were: Water Street, Cotton Tree, Joaque Bridge, Campbell Street, Brookfields, Wilberforce (for Murray Town), Signal Hill, Lumley Road (for Goderich), the Barracks (West African Regiment), P.W. Bungalow and Hill Station (for Leicester, Regent, etc).

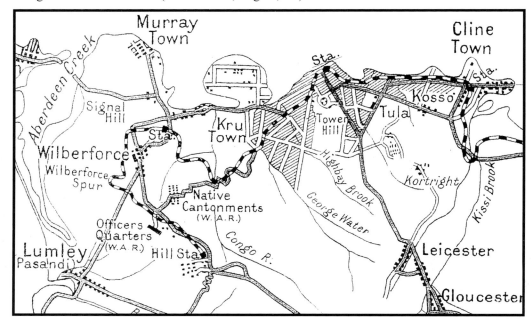

FREETOWN (WATER STREET)

2.1   The station for Hill Station trains is between the Telegraph Office (right) and the main station, which is in the background. A coach stands at the platform of the former. (T.Dickinson coll.)

XI.   The 1927 map has the main station on the right and the station for trains to Hill Station to the left of it. These departed via the curve into Charlotte Street (lower left). Locomotives off both main line and local trains used the crossover to the right of centre. The line on the left was to Government Wharf. For many years there were six branch trains each day, the first leaving here at 5.45am.

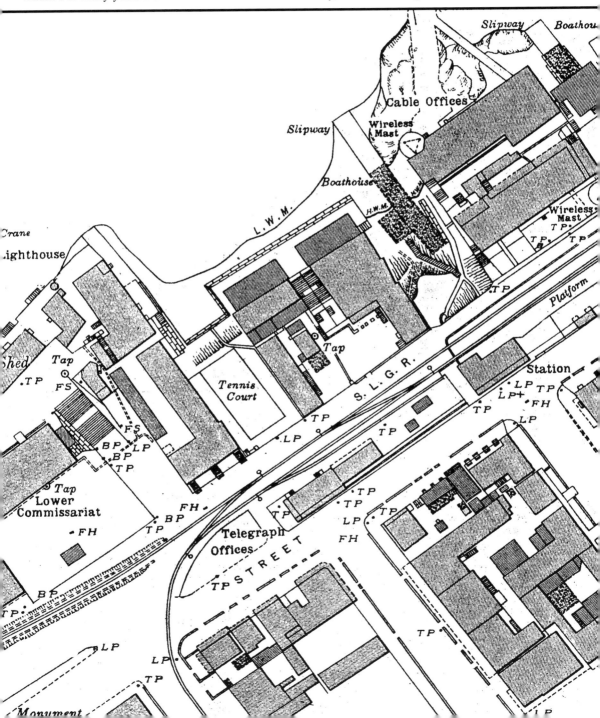

2.2   The terminal building was photographed in December 1994 when it was in use as the Government Bookshop, despite its dilapidation. In the background is the former main station, seen earlier in pictures 1.2 to 1.6. (M.Ward/R.R.Darsley coll.)

COTTON TREE

2.3   The mighty cotton tree is on the right; "the combination ticket office and waiting room was erected under it". Parts of the track were on the extreme gradient of 1 in 22. (F.Walton coll.)

2.4   Population increased rapidly with the coming of the railway and a chalet-style building was erected. Previously, transport was mostly by hammock. A half-mile long branch was opened from Brookfields to Ascension Town Cemetery in November 1907 and funeral trains were operated to it. (F.Walton coll.)

EAST OF WILBERFORCE

2.5   Trains passed over the Congo River (not the famous one) on this structure. The river is marked on map X. Records suggest that three coaches were the normal maximum. After closure, the footpath was moved on top of the bridge, which was still in use about 50 years later. It was 235ft long and had five spans. (J.Hossack coll.)

WILBERFORCE

WILBERFORCE STATION, SIERRA LEONE.

Photo., Freetown, Sierra Leone.

2.6   This 1912 franked postcard includes cable drums, suggesting that electricity had just reached the area. The first road was completed in about 1919. William Wilberforce was responsible, with others, for the abolition of the slave trade and the end of slavery itself. (R.Revell coll.)

2.7   The station was in domestic use in 1994 and the sign was serving laundry functions, while overshadowed by concrete apartments instead of palm trees. (M.Ward/R.R.Darsley coll.)

HILL STATION

2.8   This photograph is from the end of 1903 as the building was nearing completion. Lettered SLMR No. 11, the locomotive is one of the three 0-6-0Ts completed by Hunslet that year. On Boxing Day, a trial train of three coaches was operated and excursions were run on the following Easter Monday. (Royal Commonwealth Society Libary)

2.9   The chalet style building was erected, although described locally as a bungalow. In 1908 the return fare from Water Street to Hill Station was 1s 3d first class, 10d second class and 5d third class. The journey took half an hour along a scenic route. The terminus was 820ft above sea level. The first departure was often at 6.25am and the last at 6.20pm. (T.Dickinson coll.)

2.10   The other elevations are seen in 1974, by which time 3-phase current was on the poles, although the building had only single. One disadvantage of the altitude was that the rainfall exceeded 50ins in both July and August. The foreman platelayer's bungalow became the local church. (R.R.Darsley)

3. Sierra Leone Development Company

3.1   The haematite ore contained up to 57% iron and was quarried by blasting. Local labour sorted the material and tipped lumps and fines into different wagons. These were moved by hand or diesel locomotives to the top of the balance-worked inclines. (SLDC)

3.2   Two inclines are in the background, these lowering ore wagons onto the gantry from where lump material was discharged direct into main line bogie vehicles below. The fines were unloaded for screening, washing, drying and loading later. Below the top Red Ore was low grade Powder Ore, which was quarried mechanically. (SLDC)

3.3   The Powder Ore was processed in a concentrating mill from 1938 onwards. From there it was stockpiled prior to loading into wagons for conveyance to the port. The new mill in 1952 could produce 1m tons annually with 66% purity. (SLDC)

3.4   Photographs on the route are rare. This view of the Sankin Bridge was taken on 2nd May 1933, soon after its completion. Also included is a van carrying staff; there was no public traffic of any sort. Beyer Peacock supplied two 2-8-2 + 2-8-2 Garratts in 1931. (SLDC)

3.5   Two more similar Garratts followed in 1935-36. They were of the GE type, which were built in large numbers for South African Railways main lines. The first two locomotives were 0-6-0STs supplied in 1931 by Avonside for construction and shunting purposes. (SLDC)

3.6　　Wagons were unloaded at Pepel using this tippler. Up to the end of 1952, the total tonnage was 9.8m lump ore, 4.1m concentrates and 0.6m washed fines. (SLDC)

3.7 Staff transport was supplemented by Wickham railcars of which no. 75 is an example. There were over 3000 employees in the 1950s, and many were provided with housing. The company also built a 27-bed hospital. Photos 3.7 to 3.11 were taken in January 1977. This trip for visitors covered about 30 miles before the vehicle broke down. (R.T.Russell)

3.8 The railway workshops were at Pepel and the facilities were comprehensive, these included a foundry and an extensive machine shop. The SLDC constructed large power stations near both termini. (R.T.Russell)

3.9   Delivery began in March 1955 of five Sulzer 1000hp diesel-electric locomotives from the Birmingham Railway Carriage & Wagon Company. The units normally worked in pairs, back to back. (R.T.Russell)

3.10   Four Alcos came from Montreal and were recorded in the workshops, one being slightly work-weary. The overhead crane facilitated engine maintenance. The entire railway was vacuum braked from its opening. It was "mothballed" under government control in 1977 and was probably never used again commercially. (P.Rowe)

————————→

3.11   For shunting duties, three English Electric diesels arrived in March 1970. One of each type of locomotive was reported to be still on site in 1997, together with two 0-6-0 EEV diesels of two-foot gauge from the quarries. (P.Rowe)

————————→

3.12   Access by car to Pepel was difficult in 1997 as one had to drive onto a flat trolley and be pushed onto the island by local labour. This seemed to be the only operational section of railway in the country at that time. (Dr. J.Middleton/R.R.Darsley coll.)

4. Preservation

SIERRA LEONE

4.1   The former governor's coach was kept. Unlike the other wooden bodied stock, it was in good condition having usually been kept under cover. It had a bathroom, bedroom and a saloon. It displays the Sierra Leone crest used after Independence and not the one used by the governor. (R.R.Darsley)

4.2   Although part of the works area at Cline Town was retained as a factory for non-railway items after closure of the line, some part was kept for storage of items of rolling stock. Seen in 1974, this coach was converted from 1945 stock in 1961 for use by HM Queen Elizabeth II, but her visit was cancelled and it was never finished. (R.R.Darsley)

4.3   The PW trolley from Bo was another item retained to form the nucleus of a museum. It was photographed in 1994 and about 10 years later a small museum was being established in Freetown. (M.Ward/R.R.Darsley coll.)

4.4   The motive power corner included in 1997 Hudswell Clarke diesels nos 133 and 123, Beyer Peacock-Garratt no. 73 and Hunslet 2-6-2T no. 81, although this may have been initially no. 46. The CME's coach panelling had been stolen, as it was aluminium. Diesels 105 and 107 were also saved. (Dr. J.Middleton/R.R.Darsley coll.)

4.5   In another wing in 1997 was Manning Wardle 0-4-0ST no. 10 *Nellie*, along with some of the eight coaches in store. There was also one bogie guards van. The buildings were invaded in 2000 by hundreds of refugees and they left litter axle deep. (Dr. J.Middleton/R.R.Darsley)

GREAT BRITAIN

4.6   The Welshpool & Llanfair Railway purchased four coaches, in addition to no. 85. The deal was done at the 11th hour with a Lebanese scrap merchant. Unloading in Liverpool on 7th August 1975 was recorded, as one coach was being swung between the locomotive and the bridge. (P.Rowe)

4.7   Only two decades earlier, no. 85 had arrived at Liverpool from Leeds for shipping. It returned on the 7413-ton *Idomeneus* of the Elder Dempster fleet; the vessel was about five years older than the locomotive. The 3000 mile journey took two weeks. The loco had been purchased privately by two WLR members. (P.Rowe)

4.8   Low-loaders were not used for the coaches and thus a circuitous route was needed to avoid restrictive bridges. The convoy travelled via the M57, M62, M6 and A5 to reach Shrewsbury. The locomotive ran via Chester and Oswestry on a low-loader. (P.Rowe)

4.9   The coaches were reunited with rails at Castle Caereinion, the intermediate station on the WLR. The railway had previously obtained some coaches from Austria, there being few other British lines of the same gauge. (P.Rowe)

4.10   The train was reformed at Tanllan Sidings, but few passengers would be aware of their unusual source. They had been built by the Gloucester Carriage & Wagon Comany in 1961 as one 1st and three 3rd class saloons. (P.Rowe)

4.11   No. 85 was unloaded and photographed at Llanfair Caereinion. It was soon steamed and given a thorough overhaul, during which it lost its tank-top coal boxes. The SLGR stock in Wales serves as a memorial to forgotten British enterprise in Africa and the more recent initiatives involved in its repatriation. (P.Rowe)

4.12   No. 1048 was photographed in April 1977, recently outshopped. New seating was fitted but electric fans were retained, despite the lower average temperatures. (P.Rowe)

4.13   No. 85 was renumbered 14 and is seen in 1979, after a major overhaul. We hope that the photographs in this volume will help those using the SLGR stock on the WLR to visualise its former habitat. (P.Rowe)

Middleton Press

Easebourne Lane, Midhurst, W Sussex. GU29 9AZ Tel: 01730 813169 Fax: 01730 812601
Email: sales@middletonpress.co.uk www.middletonpress.co.uk
If books are not available from your local transport stockist, order direct post free UK.

BRANCH LINES
Branch Line to Allhallows
Branch Line to Alton
Branch Lines around Ascot
Branch Lines to Ashburton
Branch Lines around Bodmin
Branch Line to Bude
Branch Lines around Canterbury
Branch Lines around Chard & Yeovil
Branch Line to Cheddar
Branch Lines around Cromer
Branch Line to the Derwent Valley
Branch Lines to East Grinstead
Branch Lines of East London
Branch Lines to Effingham Junction
Branch Lines to Falmouth, Helston & St. Ives
Branch Line to Fairford
Branch Lines to Felixstow & Aldeburgh
Branch Lines around Gosport
Branch Line to Hayling
Branch Lines to Henley, Windsor & Marlow
Branch Line to Hawkhurst
Branch Line to Horsham
Branch Line to Ilfracombe
Branch Line to Kingsbridge
Branch Line to Kingswear
Branch Line to Lambourn
Branch Lines to Launceston & Princetown
Branch Lines to Longmoor
Branch Line to Looe
Branch Line to Lyme Regis
Branch Line to Lynton
Branch Lines around March
Branch Lines around Midhurst
Branch Line to Minehead
Branch Line to Moretonhampstead
Branch Lines to Newport (IOW)
Branch Lines to Newquay
Branch Lines around North Woolwich
Branch Line to Padstow
Branch Lines to Princes Risborough
Branch Lines to Seaton and Sidmouth
Branch Lines around Sheerness
Branch Line to Shrewsbury
Branch Line to Tenterden
Branch Lines around Tiverton
Branch Lines to Torrington
Branch Lines to Tunbridge Wells
Branch Line to Upwell
Branch Line to Wantage (The Wantage Tramway)
Branch Lines of West London
Branch Lines of West Wiltshire
Branch Lines around Weymouth
Branch Lines around Wimborne
Branch Lines around Wisbech

NARROW GAUGE
Austrian Narrow Gauge
Branch Line to Lynton
Branch Lines around Portmadoc 1923-46
Branch Lines around Porthmadog 1954-94
Branch Line to Southwold
Douglas to Port Erin
Douglas to Peel
Kent Narrow Gauge
Northern France Narrow Gauge
Romneyrail
Sierra Leone Narrow Gauge
Southern France Narrow Gauge
Sussex Narrow Gauge
Surrey Narrow Gauge

Swiss Narrow Gauge
Two-Foot Gauge Survivors
Vivarais Narrow Gauge

SOUTH COAST RAILWAYS
Ashford to Dover
Bournemouth to Weymouth
Brighton to Worthing
Dover to Ramsgate
Eastbourne to Hastings
Hastings to Ashford
Portsmouth to Southampton
Ryde to Ventnor
Southampton to Bournemouth

SOUTHERN MAIN LINES
Basingstoke to Salisbury
Crawley to Littlehampton
Dartford to Sittingbourne
East Croydon to Three Bridges
Epsom to Horsham
Exeter to Barnstaple
Exeter to Tavistock
London Bridge to East Croydon
Orpington to Tonbridge
Tonbridge to Hastings
Salisbury to Yeovil
Sittingbourne to Ramsgate
Swanley to Ashford
Tavistock to Plymouth
Three Bridges to Brighton
Victoria to Bromley South
Victoria to East Croydon
Waterloo to Windsor
Waterloo to Woking
Woking to Portsmouth
Woking to Southampton
Yeovil to Exeter

EASTERN MAIN LINES
Barking to Southend
Ely to Kings Lynn
Ely to Norwich
Fenchurch Street to Barking
Hitchin to Peterborough
Ilford to Shenfield
Ipswich to Saxmundham
Liverpool Street to Ilford
Saxmundham to Yarmouth
Tilbury Loop

WESTERN MAIN LINES
Banbury to Birmingham
Bristol to Taunton
Didcot to Banbury
Didcot to Swindon
Ealing to Slough
Exeter to Newton Abbot
Moreton-in-Marsh to Worcester
Newton Abbot to Plymouth
Newbury to Westbury
Oxford to Moreton-in-Marsh
Paddington to Ealing
Paddington to Princes Risborough
Plymouth to St. Austell
Princes Risborough to Banbury
Reading to Didcot
Slough to Newbury
St. Austell to Penzance
Swindon to Bristol
Swindon to Newport
Taunton to Exeter
Westbury to Taunton

MIDLAND MAIN LINES
St. Albans to Bedford
Euston to Harrow & Wealdstone
Harrow to Watford
St. Pancras to St. Albans

COUNTRY RAILWAY ROUTES
Abergavenny to Merthyr
Andover to Southampton
Bath to Evercreech Junction
Bath Green Park to Bristol
Bournemouth to Evercreech Junction
Brecon to Newport
Burnham to Evercreech Junction
Cheltenham to Andover
Croydon to East Grinstead
Didcot to Winchester
East Kent Light Railway
Frome to Bristol
Guildford to Redhill
Reading to Basingstoke
Reading to Guildford
Redhill to Ashford
Salisbury to Westbury
Stratford upon Avon to Cheltenham
Strood to Paddock Wood
Taunton to Barnstaple
Wenford Bridge to Fowey
Westbury to Bath
Woking to Alton
Yeovil to Dorchester

GREAT RAILWAY ERAS
Ashford from Steam to Eurostar
Clapham Junction 50 years of change
Festiniog in the Fifties
Festiniog in the Sixties
Festiniog 50 years of enterprise
Isle of Wight Lines 50 years of change
Railways to Victory 1944-46
Return to Blaenau 1970-82
SECR Centenary album
Talyllyn 50 years of change
Wareham to Swanage 50 years of change
Yeovil 50 years of change

LONDON SUBURBAN RAILWAYS
Caterham and Tattenham Corner
Charing Cross to Dartford
Clapham Jn. to Beckenham Jn.
Crystal Palace (HL) & Catford Loop
East London Line
Finsbury Park to Alexandra Palace
Holborn Viaduct to Lewisham
Kingston and Hounslow Loops
Lewisham to Dartford
Liverpool Street to Chingford
Mitcham Junction Lines
North London Line
South London Line
West Croydon to Epsom
West London Line
Willesden Junction to Richmond
Wimbledon to Beckenham
Wimbledon to Epsom

STEAMING THROUGH
Steaming through Cornwall
Steaming through the Isle of Wight
Steaming through Kent
Steaming through West Hants

TRAMWAY CLASSICS
Aldgate & Stepney Tramways
Barnet & Finchley Tramways
Bath Tramways
Brighton's Tramways
Bristol's Tramways
Burton & Ashby Tramways
Camberwell & W.Norwood Tramways
Clapham & Streatham Tramways
Croydon's Tramways
Dover's Tramways
East Ham & West Ham Tramways
Edgware and Willesden Tramways
Eltham & Woolwich Tramways
Embankment & Waterloo Tramways
Exeter & Taunton Tramways
Fulwell – Home to Trams, Trolleys and Buses
Great Yarmouth Tramways
Greenwich & Dartford Tramways
Hammersmith & Hounslow Tramways
Hampstead & Highgate Tramways
Hastings Tramways
Holborn & Finsbury Tramways
Ilford & Barking Tramways
Kingston & Wimbledon Tramways
Lewisham & Catford Tramways
Liverpool Tramways 1. Eastern Routes
Liverpool Tramways 2. Southern Routes
Liverpool Tramways 3. Northern Routes
Maidstone & Chatham Tramways
Margate to Ramsgate
North Kent Tramways
Norwich Tramways
Reading Tramways
Shepherds Bush & Uxbridge Tramways
Southend-on-sea Tramways
South London Line Tramways 1903-33
Southwark & Deptford Tramways
Stamford Hill Tramways
Twickenham & Kingston Tramways
Victoria & Lambeth Tramways
Waltham Cross & Edmonton Tramways
Walthamstow & Leyton Tramways
Wandsworth & Battersea Tramways

TROLLEYBUS CLASSICS
Bradford Trolleybuses
Croydon Trolleybuses
Derby Trolleybuses
Hastings Trolleybuses
Huddersfield Trolleybuses
Hull Trolleybuses
Maidstone Trolleybuses
Portsmouth Trolleybuses
Reading Trolleybuses

WATERWAY & SHIPPING
Kent and East Sussex Waterways
London to Portsmouth Waterway
Sussex Shipping - Sail, Steam & Motor
West Sussex Waterways

MILITARY BOOKS
Battle over Portsmouth
Battle over Sussex 1940
Blitz over Sussex 1941-42
Bombers over Sussex 1943-45
Bognor at War
East Ridings Secret Resistance
Military Defence of West Sussex
Military Signals from the South Coast
Secret Sussex Resistance
Surrey Home Guard

OTHER RAILWAY BOOKS
Industrial Railways of the South-East
South Eastern & Chatham Railways
London Chatham & Dover Railway
London Termini - Past and Proposed
War on the Line (SR 1939-45)